Character Education

Politeness

by Lucia Raatma

Consultant:
Madonna Murphy, Ph.D.
Professor of Education
University of St. Francis, Joliet, Illinois
Author, *Character Education in America's
Blue Ribbon Schools*

Bridgestone Books
an imprint of Capstone Press
Mankato, Minnesota

Bridgestone Books are published by Capstone Press
151 Good Counsel Drive, P.O. Box 669, Mankato, Minnesota 56002
http://www.capstone-press.com

Library of Congress Cataloging-in-Publication Data
Raatma, Lucia.
    Politeness/by Lucia Raatma.
    p. cm.—(Character education)
    Includes bibliographical references and index.
    Summary: Explains the virtue of politeness and describes ways to show politeness in
the home, school, and community.
    ISBN 0-7368-1134-6
    1. Courtesy—Juvenile literature. [1. Etiquette. 2. Conduct of life.] I. Title. II. Series.
BJ1533.C9 R33 2002
395.1′22—dc21   2001003434

Editorial Credits
Sarah Lynn Schuette, editor; Karen Risch, product planning editor; Jennifer Schonborn, cover
    production designer and illustrator; Alta Schaffer, photo researcher

Photo Credits
Capstone Press/Gary Sundermeyer, cover, 4, 6, 10, 12, 14, 16, 20
CORBIS, 18
Diane Meyer, 8

1 2 3 4 5 6 07 06 05 04 03 02

Table of Contents

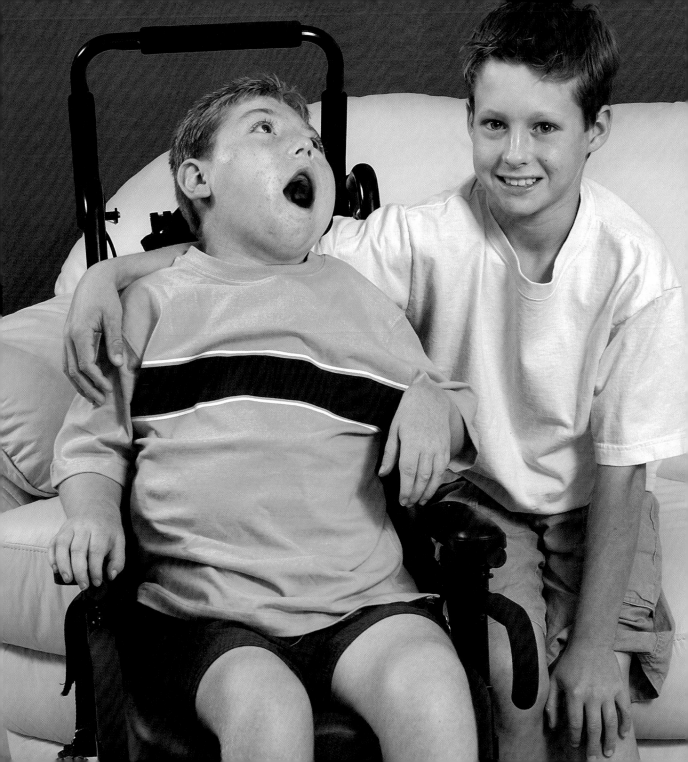

Politeness

Politeness means showing concern for others. Being polite means you treat others with kindness and respect. Politeness is showing others you care about them, their feelings, and their needs.

respect
to treat others how you would like to be treated

Being Polite

You can be polite in both your words and actions. You are polite when you say "please" and "thank you." Holding the door open for someone is a polite action.

Being Polite at Home

It is important to be polite at home. Answer the telephone politely. Take messages for family members who are not home. Be on time for meals and other family events. Give everyone a chance to talk during meals.

Politeness and Your Friends

Being polite with your friends means treating them well. Greet your friends when you meet them by asking how they are doing. It is polite to write a thank-you note to a friend who gave you a gift.

Being Polite at School

You can be polite at school by keeping your school clean. You can introduce a new student to your friends. Invite the student to play with you. Being polite also means thanking people at school when they help you.

Being Polite in Public

People notice how you act in public. A polite person is patient and waits in line. If you bump into someone, say "excuse me." Say "please" and "thank you" to store clerks, servers, and other people who help you.

Politeness in Your Community

You are polite when you respect your neighbors and their property. Turn the volume low on your stereo at night. Walk on the sidewalk and not on the grass. Remember to treat your neighbors the way you like to be treated.

property
anything that is owned by someone

"Manners are a sensitive awareness of the feelings of others. If you have that awareness, you have good manners, no matter what fork you use."
—Emily Post

Emily Post's Politeness

Emily Post wrote books in the 1920s and 1930s about having good manners. People all over the world follow her advice. She spent her life helping people treat each other well. Emily believed that politeness made everyone feel important and special.

advice
a suggestion about what someone should do

Politeness and You

It sometimes is hard to be polite. You may be angry or tired. You may feel others are not being polite to you. But you should be polite at all times. Even a smile to a new person you meet shows your politeness.

Hands On: Making Introductions

You can show politeness when you meet new people. You can practice introducing yourself and your friends with this activity.

What You Need
A friend
5 people
Classroom

What You Do
1. With a friend, walk up to two or three people in your classroom. Pretend that you do not know them very well. You can say, "Hello, my name is _____."
2. Be sure to make eye contact and smile. You may want to shake the hands of the people you are meeting.
3. Wait for them to introduce themselves to you. Then say, "It is very nice to meet you."
4. Turn to one of your friends and introduce him or her. You can say, "I would like you to meet my friend, _____."
5. Take a few minutes to talk with the people you have met. Try to learn something about them. Ask them questions about themselves.
6. When you are done talking, say good-bye to the group. You can say "It was very nice meeting you."

Words to Know

advice (ad-VICE)—a suggestion about what someone should do; Emily Post gave people advice on how to show politeness.

polite (puh-LITE)—having good manners; polite people show they care about others through their words and actions.

property (PROP-ur-tee)—anything that is owned by someone; polite people respect other people's property.

respect (ri-SPEKT)—to treat others how you would like to be treated; politeness is one way to show respect.

Read More

Doudna, Kelly. *Excuse Me.* Good Manners. Edina, Minn.: Abdo, 2001.
Oder, Ruth Shannon. *Please.* Thoughts and Feelings. Chanhassen, Minn.: Child's World, 2000.

Internet Sites

Crossroads of Character
http://library.thinkquest.org/J00l675F
Emily Post Institute–Emily Post
http://www.emilypost.com/emilypost.htm
Table Manners 101
http://www.manners101.com/TableIndex.htm

Index